RARE AND BEAUTIFUL TREASURES

KEYS TO MOVE FROM BROKENNESS TO BEAUTY

CATHERINE TOON, MD

Publishing, LLC

RARE AND BEAUTIFUL TREASURES by Catherine Toon, MD
Published by Imprint Publishing
PO Box 63125 Colorado Springs, CO 80962-3125
United States
www.catherinetoon.com
Phone: (724) 677-6801

Email: info@catherinetoon.com

All rights reserved. This book or parts thereof may not be reproduced in any form, stored in a retrieval system, or transmitted in any form by any means electronic, mechanical, photocopy, recording, or otherwise without prior written permission of the publisher, except as provided by United States of America copyright law.
Copyright © 2018 by Catherine Toon
All rights reserved.

ISBN: 978-0-9995910-2-4 (Paperback Edition)
ISBN: 978-0-9995910-4-8 (Electronic Edition)

Library of Congress Control Number - 2018901300
Printed in the United States of America
First Printing 2018

Credits and Permissions:

Scripture taken from the Holy Bible, NEW INTERNATIONAL VERSION, NIV. Copyright 1973, 1978, 1984, 2011 by Biblica, Inc. Used by permission. All rights reserved worldwide.

Scripture quotations taken from the New American Standard Bible (NASB), Copyright 1960, 1962, 1963, 1968, 1971, 1972, 1973, 1975, 1977, 1995 by The Lockman Foundation. Used by permission. www.Lockman.org

Scripture quotations taken from the Amplified Bible (AMP), Copyright 2015 by The Lockman Foundation. Used by permission. www.Lockman.org

Verses listed without translation references are partially quoted or inferred Scripture quotations taken from the Amplified Bible (AMPC), Copyright 1954, 1958, 1962, 1964, 1965, 1987 by The Lockman Foundation. Used by permission. www.Lockman.org

Scripture taken from the New King James Version. Copyright 1982 by Thomas Nelson. Used by permission. All rights reserved.

Scripture taken from The Voice. Copyright 2012 by Ecclesia Bible Society. Used by permission. All rights reserved.

Scripture taken from the King James Bible is Public domain and may be used freely, without restriction and without prior permission.

Scripture quotations are taken from the Holy Bible, New Living Translation, copyright 1996, 2004, 2007, 2013, 2015 by Tyndale House Foundation. Used by permission of Tyndale House Publishers, Inc., Carol Stream, Illinois 60188. All rights reserved.

Scripture quotations marked (TLB) are taken from The Living Bible copyright 1971. Used by permission of Tyndale House Publishers, Inc., Carol Stream, Illinois 60188. All rights reserved.

Book Cover, Interior Design, & Photography by Granite Pillar, LLC; Editing by Becky Royer.

WHAT OTHERS ARE SAYING ABOUT CATHERINE:

"Catherine Toon is a powerhouse of peace. The reflection of Jesus that shines through her and her ministry bring healing to the deepest places in hearts. You simply can't be around her without feeling the Father's perfect love. Her prophetic teaching, coaching, and healing gifts stream from the overflow of her own personal transformation and encounters with the One who loves you unconditionally and completely. You'll leave her presence knowing that you are absolutely loved, believed in, and empowered to be exactly who God created you to be."

SCHLYCE (FOUNDER OF EMERGE SCHOOL OF TRANSFORMATION)

"Catherine Toon reminds me of a mixture between the skilled surgeon that knows exactly what needs to happen to bring wholeness, mixed with the nurses that ensure you that everything is going to be ok when you're getting your first set of shots as a little boy or girl. She carries such an incredible authority, but truly operates in it to serve those people she has been entrusted with."

JUSTIN KNAPP (SENIOR LEADER AT PULSE)

"It is with high regard and sincere humility that I have the privilege of endorsing Catherine. I have known Catherine for over three years. I have monthly been a part of her life, growth, training, and

development. I have never met another person more capable to do the ministry God has called her to do. Capable in character and integrity, she has served and submitted herself to a growth (death to herself) process that few would endure. She has allowed the Lord to fashion in her His character of humility, loyalty, kindness, purity, faithfulness, and genuine beauty, in essence, the fruit of the spirit with a heart to serve and give to others more than she receives. Capable in giftedness and ability, Catherine's ability to mix the prophetic gifts she possesses (you could stop right here) with her mastery of the supernatural mind renewal prayer process is a powerful ministry of freedom and the binding of broken hearts. Capable in relationships, Catherine is proven in relationships. An honoring wife, a loved mother, an elder in the church, and a leader of leaders. I unreservedly recommend the person Catherine Toon and in so doing can also recommend the ministry that flows out of the genuineness of a life conformed to the character and image of our Lord Jesus Christ."

NATHAN BLOUSE, APOSTLE, PASTOR (SAFE PLACE MINISTRIES)

"Catherine Toon has been an amazing blessing to me and my family. She humbly flows in the prophetic, but with great accuracy. She literally prophesied something to me one day and it happened the next day just like she said. I was really amazed, but I was more comforted by the fact that I have a voice like hers in my life."

PASTOR JOE BARLOW (JOE BARLOW MINISTRIES)

By wisdom a house is built, and through understanding it is established; through knowledge its rooms are filled with rare and beautiful treasures.

Proverbs 24:3-4 (NIV)

CONTENTS

INTRODUCTION..09

1 A GOOD GOD IN A FALLEN WORLD...................11

2 STUFF HAPPENS...16

3 HIDDEN TREASURES.......................................19

4 WISDOM, UNDERSTANDING, KNOWLEDGE........22

5 CLOSING THOUGHTS......................................30

ABOUT..33

CONNECT..36

RESOURCES..37

INTRODUCTION:

This work was birthed out of a vision I had during a tumultuous time. In it, God revealed Himself as the One Who truly brings beauty for ashes.

He does not gloss over the ugly, but honors you and honors your heart.

The enemy of our souls has been defeated at the cross, but the kingdom of darkness has gotten a lot of mileage in a fallen world. We run into trouble anywhere we are not connected to God, the finished work of the cross, and what it means specifically for us. This breakdown in connection leaves wiggle room, if not an outright invitation, for the enemy to steal, kill and destroy. There is not a lick of condemnation in this, but a bracing diagnosis for how the enemy got through with his sucker punches.

However, God always has a surpassing response greater than the insult. In all the places you have not seen breakthrough in your life as you have been connecting with Him – He's not done manifesting the answer. That Answer came in the form of His Son, and the finished work of the cross. He is NOT a pat answer. And He is not an unsatisfying answer. He simply needs to be revealed.

Wherever this does not seem to be pertinent or enough, there is a lack of revelation as to what that really means for you personally, right where you are.
Love truly is the Answer, because God is a Person.

God is Love (1 John 4:8-9) and Love never fails (1 Corinthians 13:8).

Love has specific answers for you. And there is a way to get there from here – thank You, Jesus!

God wants to transform and overhaul you - your body, your family, your life, and your legacy - into something overwhelmingly powerful and strikingly beautiful!

> *By wisdom a house is built, and through understanding it is established; through knowledge its rooms are filled with rare and beautiful treasures.*
> *(Proverbs 24:3-4, NIV)*

So buckle up your seatbelts.
It's time to encounter God.
It's time to encounter the One Who triumphed so that YOU can triumph!

It is time to see the beauty of His treasures!

And that is my heart and prayer for you!
-Catherine

CHAPTER 1 – A GOOD GOD IN A FALLEN WORLD

We hear it all the time – some senseless tragedy amidst the backdrop of the ongoing tragedies of war, starvation, murder, abuse, the sex trade, pollution, fallen leaders, family demolishment, addictions… you name it.

We live in fallen world. The scent of it rises up, threatening to mar the beauty that is around us.

As believers, we are admonished to retreat back to a loving good God, Who has answers and Who is the Answer. And this is the right response.

Jesus knew about suffering. He admonished His disciples (and us, as His disciples), in John 16:32-33 (AMP):

> *Take careful notice: an hour is coming, and has arrived, when you will all be scattered, each to his own home, leaving Me alone; and yet I am not alone, because the Father is with Me. 33 I have told you these things, so that in Me you may have [perfect] peace. In the world you have tribulation and distress and suffering, but be courageous [be confident, be undaunted, be filled with joy]; I have overcome the world." [My conquest is accomplished, My victory abiding.]*

Now at the time when Jesus was crucified, a crushed, scorned man on a cross did not look like victory. Even a resurrected Savior on the third day did not immediately bring down corrupt political systems and the injustice of an oppressed people.

Not many of the people who are drawn to this book would outwardly accuse Jesus of not being good. But here we are – a good God and a fallen world.

What the heck, Jesus?! Right?

Just as a disclaimer, in no way am I going to fully unpack the presence of evil in a world created by ultimate good. More brilliant minds than my own have debated this issue throughout the ages.

However, in the midst of this mystery, there are some things to grab ahold of and a Person Who can grab ahold of you in all the hellish storms you are going through. In the end, if the answer is not complete – the Answer still has more to say. You may be in the middle of what seems to be silence or a pause. This is because there is more God has in response that has not manifested or been unveiled yet.

God and His true nature and the vast extent of His goodness has been veiled. In my book, *Marked by Love,* I spend significant time investigating the struggle we have with seeing Him rightly. This is an honest struggle. The true nature of God has been veiled by the Law and the spirit of legalism (religion) that operates through it (2 Corinthians 3;13-16; 4:3-4).

Jesus came to tear the veil that separated us from Him, symbolized by the Jewish Temple veil that was torn after His crucifixion.

2 Corinthians 3:15-17 (NIV) says:

> *Even to this day when Moses is read, a veil covers their hearts. 16 But whenever anyone turns to the Lord, the veil is taken away. 17 Now the Lord is the Spirit, and where the Spirit of the Lord is, there is freedom.*

As a matter of fact, He is so good that He allowed His flesh to be torn so that we could enter into union with God and the freedom that comes with it (Hebrews 10:19-21).

Many of us have a lurking sense that Jesus is the kind, loving, and gentle member of the godhead, while Father God is good, but somewhere He has a scary, vengeful streak. However, the Word of God says that Jesus is the *express image* of the Father (Hebrews 1:3). Jesus even said, if you have seen Him, you have seen the Father (John 14:7,9).

James 1:16-17 (AMP) says:

> *Do not be misled, my beloved brothers and sisters. 17 Every good thing given and every perfect gift is from above; it comes down from the Father of lights [the Creator and Sustainer of the heavens], in whom there is no variation [no rising or setting] or shadow cast by His turning [for He is perfect and never changes].*

Look at verse 16. It is easy to be misled in our hearts, if not our intellects. Bad things accuse a good God of being uncaring, distant, preoccupied or wimpy. satan (small "s" because he is not worth capitalizing) and the entire kingdom of darkness is constantly accusing God and accusing us. And because of bad things that happen and good things that haven't, we can emotionally, in our natural state, sometimes end up accusing God in our hearts or subconscious minds.

But God is completely and utterly good and He simply does not change (James 1:17, Hebrews 13:8). He cannot be otherwise at any time, because God is Love (1 John 4:8,16):

> *Whoever does not love does not know God, because God is love. 16 And so we know and rely on the love God has for us. God is love. Whoever lives in love lives in God, and God in them.*

Love describes Himself in 1 Corinthians 13:4-7.

Love is patient, love is kind. It does not envy, it does not boast, it is not proud. 5 It does not dishonor others, it is not self-seeking, it is not easily angered, it keeps no record of wrongs. 6 Love does not delight in evil but rejoices with the truth. 7 It always protects, always trusts, always hopes, always perseveres.

And at the end of the whole passage, in verse 8, He drops a bombshell:

Love never fails.

CHAPTER 2 – STUFF HAPPENS

Okay. *Love never fails* (1 Corinthians 13:8).

Did you get that?
The imperishable Person Who is Truth said He never fails.
Love has committed Himself by His own Word.

As a matter of fact, He says He upholds *all things* by the Word of His power. That is to say, that if He were to go back upon His Word, the universe would implode. Now that's commitment!

I can hear the "yeah-buts":

What about all the stuff that has happened?
What about my baby that died?
What about my business that failed?
What about my bankruptcy?
What about my addiction?
What about all the starving kids in _____?
What about the sex trade?

So, what about it, Jesus?

I was talking to Him about this because these are really good questions. And Love has no qualms about such authentic discussions. The question really boils down to, "Who is responsible for evil?" It wasn't God's will for humankind to fall and bring down the earth with it. Bad things happen all the time and it is *not* God's will.

2 Peter 3:8-9 (NIV) says:

> *But do not forget this one thing, dear friends: With the Lord a day is like a thousand years, and a thousand years are like a day. 9 The Lord is not slow in keeping his promise, as some understand slowness. Instead he is patient with you, not wanting anyone to perish, but everyone to come to repentance.*

What we see from this passage, unlike what popular Christianity often touts, God is not in control of everything. Since people die and go to hell, clearly, His will does not always come to pass.

He doesn't coerce or force people to do good or not to do bad. In Genesis 1:26,28, He gave humankind dominion over the earth and everything on the earth. But on that note, He didn't give humankind dominion over *one another*. There is a word for that kind of manipulation and control and it is called witchcraft.

Jesus was given all authority (Matthew 28:18, Philippians 2:10), and He gave us His authority to use because He gave us His name (Luke 10:19, John 14:13-14, 15:16, 16:23-24, 17:2) to expand the kingdom of God. We often do not realize what we have or know how to use it.

The enemy, with his sucker punches, does get through at times. He roams like a roaring lion and seeks someone who he can devour (1 Peter 5:8-9). That means there are times when people are vulnerable, and he has a measure, sometimes a huge measure, of success because we fail to resist him. Either we don't know we can, we don't know how, or we simply don't do/forget to do what we know to do. But folks, with all that, let me say, it is NOT OVER 'till it's over. Jesus is Lord over the impossible (Matthew 17:20, Matthew 19:26, Mark 9:23, 10:27, 14:36; Luke 1:37).

God's has a perspective that bad things are actually only temporary. 2 Corinthians 4:17-18 (NIV) says:

> *For our light and momentary troubles are achieving for us an eternal glory that far outweighs them all. 18 So we fix our eyes not on what is seen, but on what is unseen, since what is seen is temporary, but what is unseen is eternal.*

You see, one way or the other, Love gets to have the last word. One way or the other - Love never fails!

CHAPTER 3 - HIDDEN TREASURES

Stuff has happened to me.
Stuff has happened to you.

I was sexually abused since before I had speech to be able to formulate word-framed memories. I had buried that for years, even as it haunted me. At age 27, I started having flashbacks of it.

One night I had a vision:

> God showed me, as my adult self, in an old, beautiful 3-story home, walking in the upper floors. But something was terribly wrong and menacing. I could not put my finger on it. I was drawn to the lowest basement floor and there was a room that I knew to be a little girl's room. I did NOT want to go in there. But I was compelled. As I opened the door of the light pink room, the scene looked as if a bomb that had gone off. Thick dust was settling everywhere. There was a large pile of rubble in the middle of the room with blood splattered here and there. On top of

the rubble were the remains of a little girl. Nothing was really left of her, except a face with no mouth and two large blue eyes - tears streaming down them. In the closet was the perpetrator laughing. "AHHHHHH!" I slammed the door and ran up the stairs. I bolted up out of my sleep. I knew this little girl was me. I was a wreck for 3 days. My husband was on deployment and it was all I could do to take care of my two little girls. I clung onto Jesus. On the third day (the irony not lost on me), Papa spoke, "Catherine, what do you see?" I looked with my spiritual eyes and saw the same room again. But this time it was COMPLETELY spotless. Everything evil and destructive was gone without a trace. The room was totally empty, pink, but oh-so shiny. As I continued to look, the glory of the Lord engulfed the whole scene. And then Papa said to me, "Let's fill it with beautiful things!"

And He has been filling me and filling my life with beautiful things ever since – THANK YOU, Lord!!!

> *By wisdom a house is built, and through understanding it is established; 4 through knowledge its rooms are filled with rare and beautiful treasures."*
> *(Proverbs 24:3-4, NIV)*

and provide for those who grieve in Zion — to bestow on them a crown of beauty instead of ashes, the oil of joy instead of mourning, and a garment of praise instead of a spirit of despair. They will be called oaks of righteousness, a planting of the Lord for the display of his splendor.

(Isaiah 61:3, NIV)

CHAPTER 4 – WISDOM, UNDERSTANDING AND KNOWLEDGE

THE GOD GOODS

So, according to God's Word, we have access to beauty, joy, praise, righteousness, splendor, and treasures. But a promise needs feet on the ground, so to speak, to fulfill itself.

The Word of God says all God's promises are yes and amen (2 Corinthians 1:20). That means they were His idea in the first place, so we don't have to convince Him. We are the ones who probably need convincing. We don't have to, and shouldn't, beg like slaves and paupers when we are royal kids.

He doesn't hold out on us. If He gave us Himself as a sacrifice in Christ, what lesser thing would He *possibly* withhold from us (Romans 8:32)? He provides everything by grace through faith.

Grace means He freely gives us all things He sacrificed for on the cross. That means it's free with NO STRINGS ATTACHED. Isaiah 53:4-5 outlines what that cross thing covered:

- Forgiveness of ALL sin for ALL time and for ALL the world so that we could be made His righteousness. His righteousness is our righteousness as a gift, not something we pump up or earn (2 Corinthians 5:21, Ephesians 2:8, Hebrews 10:12,1 Timothy 2:6; 1 John 2:2).

- Forgiveness of iniquity (the tendency to sin; Isaiah 53:4-5)

- Everything to obtain our peace or the Hebrew word, "shalom" translated as:
  completeness (in number)
  safety
  soundness (in body)
  welfare
  health
  prosperity
  peace, quiet, tranquility, contentment in all areas (including relationships)

- Healing or the word, "râphâ" which means:
  to mend (by stitching)

>   to cure
>   to (cause to) heal
>   to physician
>   to repair thoroughly
>   to make whole

And the Word of God says all this is in *past tense* (2 Peter 2:24). His Word also says that that He *already* has given us ALL THINGS for life and godliness (2 Peter 1:3).

All the goodies belong to His kids by inheritance at His expense. This is because He is a good Daddy, and He couldn't help Himself. And He does not write you out of His will when you misbehave. He is pleased with you, even in your mess, because He did what it took to bring you back to Himself. This is true even if you are silly enough to reject Him.

He doesn't disown His kids when we foolishly disown Him. He doesn't change (Romans 10:16). He keeps His goodies in store for us. They may be hidden, but they are not hidden *from* us, they are hidden *for* us!

We can choose to become enemies of Him *in our minds*, because we want to cling on to sin. But He is *not*, and *never was*, our enemy (Colossians 1:21). He is clear about who the enemy is – and it is NOT His kids. We need to be clear who the enemy is as well!

Even if we reject Him, His privileges are waiting for us (Romans 8:32, 1 Timothy 6:17). They are available by His grace and accessed through faith. This faith we don't need to muster up, work up, confess up or fake up. He knows we do not have it in and of ourselves. So, as the Provider, He provides faith, through His Word and through His Spirit. His Spirit unveils who He really is, what He really accomplished on that cross, and reveals the true Gospel (Romans 4:16, 10:16-18; 1 Corinthians 12:9, Ephesians 2:8).

WISDOM, UNDERSTANDING, KNOWLEDGE

So how do we access all this beauty, joy, praise, righteousness, splendor, and treasures?

The Word of God says that we receive His goodness and goods by grace. He provided that grace and IS grace. We access that grace through faith, which He also provides (Romans 4:16, Ephesians 2:8, Romans 10:16-18).

He is all in and holding nothing back (Romans 8:32).

Where we fall short, is that we simply fail to see Him as good as He is. There is no condemnation in this – it is simply not allowed (Romans 8:1). But it is diagnostic. We struggle to believe that He lavishly provides for EVERYTHING we need and desire, in ways that we can handle. This "in ways we cannot handle" is not a cop-out or a loophole. Case in point – if $100,000,000 would cause you to run amok and self-destruct, He is not going to provide something you can't handle. He's a GOOD Daddy.

There is a way to walk all this out. God is not a tease or a sadist. There is wisdom and understanding to get there from here. There is knowledge of Him and all He has provided.

You see, Wisdom is Person (Proverbs 1:20). And there is a way to operate in the faith His Gospel provides. The Gospel literally means "good news". But the spirit of man's religion causes us to focus on what we have "to do" vs. what He *already* did for us. It is exhausting. It makes the Gospel a starting point, but then it is "up to us" to clean up ourselves and grunt it out. But God, Who IS Love, as well as Wisdom and Truth (1 John 4:8-9, Proverbs 1:20, John 14:6), says that apart from Him – from vital ongoing union with Him, you can do NO THING (John 15:4-5).

We need His help to KNOW Him accurately and intimately – that is where His grace and peace is multiplied (2 Peter 1:2). We need His understanding in order to understand Him and know what we have access to. And we need His wisdom with what that looks like, to walk it all out, so that all His promises are actually fulfilled.

Isn't it awesome, and no coincidence, that He is called Comforter, Counselor, Helper, Advocate, Intercessor, Strengthener, Standby (John 14:15,26; 15:26; 16:17)? Check it out in the Amplified Version – it will make you happy! He knows that we are totally unable to help ourselves, in and of ourselves. We are totally dependent upon Him, and He's masterful at His job. He gets to do all the heavy lifting!

John 15:5 (AMP) says:

> *I am the Vine; you are the branches. The one who remains in Me and I in him bears much fruit, for [otherwise] apart from Me [that is, cut off from vital union with Me] you can do nothing.*

Matthew 11:28-29 (AMPC) says:

> *Come to Me, all you who labor and are heavy-laden and overburdened, and I will cause you to rest. [I will ease and relieve and refresh your souls.] 29 Take My yoke upon you and learn of Me, for I am gentle (meek) and humble (lowly) in heart, and you will find rest (relief and ease and refreshment and recreation and blessed quiet) for your souls.*

And He will even help you when you struggle to believe He really is that good (Mark 9:24). You can ride upon His faith – His confidence that He's really got this. He's a happy God and wants happy, carefree kids (1 Peter 5:7). Carefree kids reflect really good parents!

The Word of God says that the "fear (or reverence) of the Lord" is the beginning of wisdom (Proverbs 1:7, 9:10). That means He is a big - "G" God, and we are not. We are His beloved powerful kids. We were made in His image and likeness, to kick enemy butt and take names in His name. But we do so in rest, knowing that He's got our backs.

We are called to release problems that are God-sized to Him, to let Him be amazing on our behalf. We let Him do His thing for us by not insisting on trying to handle our issues independently. We are to depend upon Him, and live and have our being in Him. And in Him is everything you could ever possibly want in your heart of hearts and in your wildest of dreams. And it is there in crazy abundance (Ephesians 3:20, 1 Timothy 6:17).

He is holding nothing back – He's just after your heart FIRST so He can safely give you all those fabulous things (Matthew 6:33).

Idols destroy people (Psalm 106:36), and He will not give you things that will destroy you. He is Love and an astoundingly good Papa!

He is after your heart.
He is after intimacy.

In this place, we are dependent upon Him every step of the way. We are safe, free, carefree, extravagantly provided for, and ridiculously powerful!

He is able to make up for the years that have been ravaged, destroyed, defiled and stolen (Joel 2:25-26).

He is able to fill every room of your heart and your life with rare and exquisitely beautiful treasures!

CHAPTER 5 – CLOSING THOUGHTS

And so, we are back to where we started.

> *"By wisdom a house is built, and through understanding it is established; 4 through knowledge its rooms are filled with rare and beautiful treasures."*
> *(Proverbs 24:3-4, NIV)*

God is Love and He not only cares about the things you have lost, but He is able, and frankly, pumped, to recompense you. You are His child in whom He is delighted, despite your issues. Your issues do not define you – He defines you!

He has glorious treasures of all sorts stored up for you *right here and now* (Hebrews 11:1). And everything is found in Him.

He will help you unlock them as you connect with the rooms of His heart for you! He is Love!

And this is my prayer:

That your mind, imagination and understanding would be

enlightened...

- That you may know, experience and walk out for yourself the hope of Love's calling for you personally.

- That you would know and experience the riches "of you" and the glory of the inheritance Love has placed inside of you.

- That you would know the exceeding greatness of Love's power on your behalf.

- And mostly, that you would intimately experience the love of Christ, which surpasses knowledge, that you would be filled with all the fullness of Love, Himself.

In Jesus's name – Amen!!

Love,

Catherine

SHARE YOUR TESTIMONY:

Send me a note at: info@catherinetoon.com

ABOUT CATHERINE:

As an MD in residency, Catherine's life was radically transformed when she had a powerful and personal encounter with Jesus. The Jesus Catherine met that day was the real deal, the same Jesus Who is described in the Bible as a loving, intimate, kind, and accessible miracle worker.

As Catherine developed her relationship with Jesus and grew in her love and trust of Him, He tenderly walked her out of the intense sorrow, suffering, and heavy bondage that had resulted after years of childhood abuse. In the process, Holy Spirit became her very best friend.

Along the way, the Father birthed a burning desire and deep conviction within her heart that He had plans to use her powerfully to help others experience the same Jesus she had come to know so intimately. He would heal and restore others through her in the same way He had healed and restored her. After four years of practice as a board-certified Internist, she retired from medicine to raise her children and wholeheartedly pursue God's call on her life.

In 2007, by divine connection, she met Schlyce Jimenez, Rethink LLC and Emerge School of Transformation's Founder, while attending Charis Bible College. She has been an integral part of Schlyce's life. She birthed and directed prayer, prophetic, and healing room ministries. In 2011, Catherine spearheaded bringing Sozo, an inner healing ministry, and what would become known as Encounter Ministries, to Prayer Mountain, CO. Shortly thereafter, she launched and oversaw monthly Encounter Weekends at the ministry's headquarters, Prayer Mountain, CO, overseeing the Sozo, Prophetic, Healing, Dream Interpretation, Healing Massage, Prophetic Portrait Photography, and Recreational Encounter Teams.

Catherine was officially licensed by Schlyce in February of 2011, and ordained as an Apostle and Prophet by her in February of 2015. Over the years, Catherine has written multiple curricula, teachings, and blogs. She has an anointed, powerful, thorough, and prophetic teaching style. As a powerful prophetic intercessor, who regularly operates in the miraculous, Catherine's prophetic ministry is sought out by leaders and entrepreneurs from around the globe. Her prophetic voice is acutely accurate in speaking forth vision, direction, confirmation, and practical strategic insight into individuals, leaders, organizations, and businesses. She served as the Director of the Emerge Campus School of Transformation program in Woodland Park, CO, which is designed to help students reach their full potential in Christ through transformational teaching, activations, Rapid Mind Renewal sessions, and much more. She also directed The Transformation Center.

After years of ministry partnership with Schlyce, Catherine was released to launch forward globally, fulfilling her heart's desire to touch the entire planet. In 2016, she founded catherinetoon.com and Imprint LLC, a company that is dedicated to restoring wholeness, revealing identity, and releasing destiny to this generation through the unveiling of God's imprint of love uniquely expressed in every person.

She released her first book, Marked by Love, in May 2017, which takes the reader on a wild encounter with God as Love to discover their true identity, through the lens of the imprint placed upon every person by God, the Lover of our souls. Because of the book's wonderful reception, she followed up with a Marked by Love online course and workbook in the Spring of 2018.

Catherine lives in Colorado, enjoying life with her husband, Brian, and her powerhouse children, Veronica, Rachel, and Robert.

For more information about Catherine Toon and Imprint, see www.catherinetoon.com.

CONNECT:

catherinetoon.com

Receive weekly videos direct to your inbox.
Sign up @
catherinetoon.com

FOLLOW:

 @CatherineToonMD

 catherinetoon

 @CatherineToonMD

 Catherine Toon, MD

 Catherine Toon

REQUEST:

If you would like Catherine to speak at your event or more intimate gathering, contact us at:
info@catherinetoon.com

RARE AND BEAUTIFUL TREASURES

RESOURCES:

MARKED BY LOVE

ONLINE COURSE

Experience God in ways you never thought possible

For more information on the *Marked by Love Online Course* or *Marked by Love* book go to catherinetoon.com

RARE AND BEAUTIFUL TREASURES

www.ingramcontent.com/pod-product-compliance
Lightning Source LLC
Chambersburg PA
CBHW071803040426
42446CB00012B/2694